M000281945

Inspiration
For The Choir

Devotions For Rehearsals

Fred H. Wilkins

CSS Publishing Company, Inc., Lima, Ohio

INSPIRATION FOR THE CHOIR

For more information about CSS Publishing Company resources, visit our website at www.csspub.com.

ISBN 0-7880-1848-5
                                        PRINTED IN U.S.A.

The devotions for church choirs which appear on the following pages are dedicated to the hundreds of singers who have been musically influenced by Dr. Fred H. Wilkins for more than fifty years. They come from the churches in the State of California as follows:

Our Saviour's Lutheran Church, Long Beach

Ascension Lutheran Church, Rancho Palos Verdes

Christ the King Lutheran Church, Torrance

Community Presbyterian Church, South Gate

First Methodist Church, Gardena

First Lutheran Church, Inglewood

Saint Mark's Community Methodist Church, Los Angeles

Chapel, United States Naval Hospital, San Diego

Epworth Methodist Church, Los Angeles

The author is deeply indebted to Adelyn Johnson of Long Beach, California, for her editing of the manuscript.

Special thanks go to the Chancel Choir of Our Saviour's Lutheran Church of Long Beach, California, for "trying out" these devotions during their choir year, 1997-1998, and for their encouraging comments.

Introduction

The choir director is responsible for the spiritual leadership of his singers as he directs their attention to God, always singing to His honor and glory, never a performance for the audience!

It is suggested that the devotions which are included in this volume be presented at the opening of the rehearsal in order to set the tone, mood, and/or attitude for the practice period. This could take the form of the director personally reading the devotion, or by electing or appointing a choir chaplain who would be responsible for selecting, in turn, each of the members of the choir to lead the weekly devotion.

While devotions may have been suggested for each weekly rehearsal throughout the choir's year, one might wish to go in any order. Some editing may be necessary to meet specific situations in various local churches.

It is the author's hope that all choirs using this volume will indeed be blessed and drawn closer to our Lord Jesus, the Christ.

Admonition

Ephesians 5:1-2, 19-20

Do as God does. After all, you are his dear children.

Let love be your guide. Christ loved us and offered his life for us as a sacrifice that pleases God.

When you meet together, sing psalms, hymns, and spiritual songs, as you praise the Lord with all your heart.

Always use the name of our Lord Jesus Christ to thank God the Father for everything. Amen.

Table Of Contents

VI — Closing Of The Choir Season

VII — Closing Devotions

VIII — Orders Of Worship

Preparation For Prayer

- Place your feet flat on the floor.

- Let your hands fall loosely in your lap.

- Close your eyes.

- Focus on your breathing.

- Very slowly, take five deep breaths.

- Each time as you exhale, let out any and all of the tension which you may be feeling in your body.

- Now just breathe normally.

- Allow yourself to become deeply aware of your individual body parts: your heart, your mind, and your soul.

- Just let go.

- Center your thoughts on God dwelling within you.

- Be at peace.

- Let this be a very special time for you to communicate with God.

- Take a few moments now for silent prayer.

- Amen.

- Open your eyes, look around you, smile at someone, give him or her a hug.

- Laugh together.

I. Opening Of The Choir Season

September
Date used: _____
By: _____

1 — Choir Dedication

Oh, is it "choir dedication" time again? Doesn't Mary, our choir director, know that we are committed to doing this service? In the first place, if we weren't so dedicated, we wouldn't be here every week.

Then Jim spoke up — remember the tenor with the big mouth? — every choir has one. "I like the fact that the pastor calls us up to the altar each fall. For me at least, it reminds me of a promise that I am going to set aside every Thursday evening and every Sunday morning to commit this time to the Lord. I know that promises are made to be broken; that's why I like the terms 'commitment' and 'dedication.' "

"Well said, Jim." That was our pastor speaking. "We install our church officers at the altar at the beginning of the fiscal year, and we dedicate our Sunday school teachers each fall.

"It seems to me only appropriate that our singers who are here forty weeks out of the Christian year should begin their year by being blessed by God for the service they are committing to do. Better still, with each of these installations, it reminds the congregation of the number of our members who work so hard week by week so that this congregation can make a statement to this community."

Let us pray:
In this tabernacle, O God, may we all meet you and your Son, Jesus, the Christ. As we come to the banquet, let us celebrate Jesus' life and death. We want to learn from him so that we may follow in his footsteps.

Since we are ministers of music and worship, help us to lead others: members and friends of the congregation, visitors and total

11

strangers. May we give them the message that there are people here to listen, to comfort, and to be their friend. This is the message of your love; allow others to meet you through us, His servants. Bless us now as we sing. Amen.

2 — Emotion

In our reading of the Psalms of David, we are reminded of his encouragement to *sing unto the Lord!*

If you haven't sung an anthem with a tear in your eye or a lump in your throat lately, you've missed the big picture. This is your year to break out in "goose bumps" occasionally: either because the music speaks to your highest musical values, training, and experience, or because you have allowed your heart strings to vibrate in rhythm with the composer's. We can't be expected to feel everything the same, for we are all so grossly different.

As an individual choir singer, I would like to charge you this evening to be highly conscious of God:

- singing through you, and
- speaking to His people in the congregation through you.

Also:

- to have the consciousness of Christ, the sense of God within you, and
- to have the mind of Christ guiding and directing you.

And in doing all of this with joy in your heart:

- celebrating how much God loves you and cares about you,
- acknowledging how generous He has been in bestowing talent upon you,
- thanking Him for blessing you with a gorgeous voice, with fine musical ability, and
- allowing Him to inspire you to develop your talent as far as you can go.

Truly, we are richly blessed; we have received in large measure. If our service is a burden, something is wrong in our perception of where we stand in our relationship to God. This is not to say that our entire lives should revolve around the church choir. After all, God knows we are mothers and fathers, sons and daughters, grandparents, teachers, physicians, lawyers, engineers, secretaries, office managers, printers, chemists, homemakers, retired folks, nurses — even a psychologist thrown in here and there — and lots more.

What I feel that He asks of us, is that we give our all *when* we can come to rehearsals and to services. Obviously, not everyone can come every week in any choir. I feel He asks us to be open to learn, to grow, but most important, *to experience!* When we feel something from our involvement with the choir, we hope we will leave our rehearsals and services as changed persons: enlarged in spirit, calmer, more at peace. Wouldn't it be great if we even became more loving? We demonstrate our faith when we are committed to reaching out for others, more accepting of whom, how, and what others may be, and more accepting of ourselves, too. It is especially critical that we accept ourselves.

I would hope that we would really pay attention to the texts of what we sing — to let the depth of meaning of the words reach the very marrow of our bones — to feel God speaking to us through the right side of our brains — the emotional side where we allow insight and inspiration to begin to change our lives.

But be careful! You may leave such a changed person that you may find your negativity decreasing, you may laugh more easily, the smiles may come more often and stay a little longer. You may even feel like giving of yourself and receiving from others in lots of new ways. It could be really dangerous! And then, not knowing what else to do, you would be absolutely free to come back next week and celebrate all over again the tremendously wonderful person that you are as God's very special creation.

As we have the "love-in" with God, with ourselves, and with one another, God in all His wisdom will surely give us power, strength, direction, and blessing all the days of our lives for *this is dwelling in the house of the Lord.*

Let us pray:
We are yours, O God. Take us and use us for Jesus' sake. Amen.

September
Date used: _____
By: _____

3 — Robes

By the time I started singing in the adult choir as a boy of thirteen, robes were the required "uniform of the day." The ladies were not permitted to wear earrings of any sort or corsages, even if it was Mother's Day.

Our sister church down the street required the men to wear black shoes, no matter the color of the suit, and the ladies had to wear plain black, closed toe and heel shoes, with a one-inch heel, no higher, no lower. And everyone processed down the main aisle in goose step, not unlike the Nazi army. Each singer had his or her own locker so that they could change before and after services.

It was hoped that this tradition would make all of the singers blend into one image — no distractions for the worshiper. Even in the rear balconies, Roman Catholics and Episcopalians alike wore their robes even on the hottest of days.

I know all of you here tonight are too young to remember, but in the late 1800s and early 1900s, things were very different. The ladies almost had a contest to see who could wear the largest hat with the most flowers and the widest brim, and the largest, most dangling earrings with the largest stones. Dresses were of every color of the rainbow and followed a host of designer styles from the catalogs of Montgomery Ward and/or Sears Roebuck. Since most choir lofts were directly behind the altar or a communion table, a visual blend of any sort was impossible.

The music was very romantic in those days with gorgeous melodies soaring through the soprano section, each singer trying to out-do all of the others with uncontrolled vibratos. Pitch and intonation were concepts unheard of. Scooping up and/or down to notes was very common. Blend and ensemble were not terms in the local church choir's vocabulary.

Thanks be to God, as we move beyond the year 2000, church music has come a long way. Most choirs process and recess, attempting to represent a congregation flowing into worship and to the altar of the Father. Dignity is preserved, but not stuffiness.

Let us pray:

As we come before you, O God, to sing your praises, we approach you with awe, wonder, and deep respect. Take away our foolish pride; help us to contain our overactive egos as we serve you in deepest humility with the voices which you have given to us. Amen.

II. Building The Church Choir

September
Date used: _____
By: _____

4 — Solos

Me, sing a solo? Solos aren't just for anyone, but it is important to remember that a solo in a worship service is very different from one in a secular concert or a musical. There is no "star" quality here.

Solos add variety to the full choir and especially to the singing of the whole congregation. Within an anthem, the solo can represent one character, as in a drama. At the very least, it can add contrast to the total fabric of the choral sound.

But not all solos are sung. Every choir needs a director, an accompanist, a librarian or two, an attendance secretary, a social chairperson to plan and arrange for the "wild parties," and a courtesy chairperson to honor birthdays, weddings, babies, retirements, and a host of other joyful occasions within the choir family. Last, but certainly not least, maybe even a president, vice-president, and treasurer. All of these folks have singular responsibilities within the choir. Solos? Yes, I think so. We must all be about our Father's business in different ways. Some of us are out in front where we are noticed, honored, praised, and even thanked. But God notices most the quiet one who works behind the scenes: all tasks are presented as a gift of love.

Let us pray:
Dear God, help us all to bring our solos to your altar — those sung and those unsung. We feel your smile as you look down upon us, blessing us as we return your gift of love. May Jesus dwell in our hearts this night and always. Amen.

5 — Numbers

Last year I was the attendance secretary. I never knew what John, our director, did with those records. At the end of the choir year in June, he used to give an award for the highest attendance. I always felt that every choir member should have gotten one. For in our choir, when all four parts were represented, it was a real blessing.

I worry about our declining numbers and I feel terrific every time a new singer "volunteers" to join us. In years past, we never sang with fewer than a full choir loft. And in our best days, we even had a waiting list, except for tenors. I guess that God just doesn't make enough of them. Do you suppose that is why they are so extraordinarily special?

John, our director, doesn't seem to worry about the number of voices we have. He just picks music that sounds great when sung by our very special group. "Where two or three are gathered together," goes the verse. This verse should be our theme for this year. Or should it be, "What we ain't got, we don't need"?

I miss the old days when we sang Handel's *Messiah* and the Brahms' *Requiem*. Once, we even sang the Bach *Mass in B-minor* with full orchestra. Those were the good ol' days. But this is the here and now. Our pastor still preaches the Word, and we sing anthems that set the mood for a closer walk with Jesus.

Let us pray:
We thank you for the resources which we have, O Heavenly Father — for every voice no matter how terrific, or how limited. But especially, Lord, we thank you for the opportunity to reach out for one more week to bring some lost soul to you. In your name, we bring the good news of the Risen Christ. Amen.

6 — Camaraderie

There is such a joy when we come together as Christians to complete a work project or to have a social event. At each of these gatherings we know that Christ is present because that was, and is, his promise. I guess that includes choir practice, too.

One of the things that I like about this choir is the amount of help I receive from other singers in my section. This is only my second year in a choir. Jane, my partner — I always lean on her — has been singing in this choir for over twenty years. Before that, she sang in high school and college choirs.

I would encourage all of you to ask for help. If you lose your place, ask; if you can't figure out the clef signs, ask. I always get confused with D.S. (*dal segno* — repeat from the sign) and D.C. (*da capo* — repeat from the beginning). For a long time, I thought our director, Sam, was talking about Del Taco. I didn't know what he meant, but suddenly I realized that I was getting hungry.

Then there's the funny "S" with the line and dots. First ending, second ending, alternate ending! Wow! Now I'm really lost. But I just ask Jane, who seems to know everything. Then I write myself a little note in English right on the music. By Sunday, I'm no longer confused. Thank God for the Janes and Sams in this choir who keep me from getting lost.

Let us pray:
You lead us through the maze of this journey which we call life, O Lord, by giving us guideposts or signs to make our paths clear. We lean on you for your guidance to see us through, and for your wisdom and strength. We follow in the steps of Jesus because he is our Master. Bless us this evening as we sing your praises. Amen.

19

7 — Think Big

Recently, while on vacation, the pastor in the small mission church which I visited, preached on Jesus' feeding of the 5,000 with the two fish and the five small loaves of bread. His illustration was a quote from the great evangelist, the Reverend Moody, from The Moody Bible Institute. He said, "If God is your partner, *think big!*"

This philosophy could be applied to any congregation whose mission is to send out missionaries (every member of the congregation is a missionary) to go and minister to the unchurched. *Think big!*

Choirs, too, need to grow in numbers to replace those who move away, those who become ill, and perhaps even those who just burn out or even die. As every member of the choir sees himself/herself as being on the Choir Recruitment Committee, then every phone call and every handshake can include an invitation to "Come, join us as we sing unto the Lord!" We may not even have room in our choir loft for the 375-voice Mormon Tabernacle Choir, but whatever number of seats we do have, they will not fill to capacity until we begin to *think big!*

Let us pray:

Dear God, with the Reverend Moody we declare, "You are our partner." Forgive us for being shortsighted in the past, for having too little faith, and even, at times for being too lazy to reach out for others to come with us to sing your praises.

Fresh and revitalized, we make a new commitment right now to *think big* — to demonstrate our concern for others, not only for the help they can give us by singing in this choir, but for the blessing we know they will receive by singing your praises all the day long. In Jesus' name we pray. Amen.

8 — Count

In basic training in the military, a soldier or a sailor is taught to count in order that he/she might be in step with the other members of his/her company.

In choral or instrumental musical groups, conductors have been known to yell, "When all else fails, ladies and gentlemen, *count!*" We hope this permits the musician, and singers are musicians, to come in at the right time and to stop singing at the right time.

According to Webster, *count* means:
- to add up
- to reach a total
- to include
- to be taken into account
- to rely on, to depend on
- a reckoning

In a broader sense, *count* means:
- to have importance or a specified value

To count for something suggests that we were all blessed by God when the little drop of semen fertilized the egg and we were born with value, worth, dignity, specialness, talent, creativity, and the list goes on. We claim that heritage this very night as we gather to develop our talents and learn to sing His praises more beautifully and effectively.

Not that God is keeping score, but should there be an accounting or a reckoning when we greet Saint Peter at the pearly gates, our commitment to Almighty God and His service of worship is measured by our presence here this evening and every rehearsal and service for the years passed and the years to come.

Just as God is counting on us, let us count on each other for encouragement, support, help, and inspiration.

21

Let us pray:

Dear God, please accept our commitment of our musical talents to your services of worship. Take our gifts and develop them to the highest level possible, all for your honor and glory. In Jesus' name we pray. Amen.

III. Improving The Choir's Technique

November
Date used: _____
By: _____

9 — Diaphragm

"Get in touch with your diaphragm," shouts Ken, our director. "Flex the muscles so that the air will spin slowly, evenly, and smoothly out of the lungs. When your diaphragm is working, it puts intensity into your tone; then the vibrating sound floats to the back pew. Otherwise, you are working too hard and the choral tone is not as beautiful as it could be."

Ken was always saying stuff like that. He must have read a book or something. I never quite knew what he meant, but when I stopped singing and just listened, I could actually hear the sound change and improve. It was beautiful — almost magic.

When I got home, I looked up the word "diaphragm" in the dictionary. There was even a picture demonstrating how it moves. It said, "The muscle partition between the chest and the abdominal cavity."

Then I got to thinking, "That's what God does for us." He puts the intensity into our lives. He gives us a purpose for being on this planet. His muscle causes our lives to intensify, to vibrate in conjunction with our fellow Christians to bring beauty and wholeness to this world. As my college professor used to say, "He makes us dynamos to be set in motion to follow His Son's teachings and to proclaim Jesus to the unchurched."

Let us pray:
Our loving Heavenly Father, we want to be useful in your kingdom. Help us to sing with beauty of tone as we bring your Word to this congregation. Use us also away from this hallowed tabernacle to be witnesses to Jesus' birth and resurrection. In the secret places of our hearts and minds, whisper or, if necessary, shout to us those things which we are to do in this coming week to spread the gospel to everyone with whom we come in contact. We give you all of the praise and the glory. In Jesus' name we pray. Amen.

10 — Diction

"Explode the final consonants, cross the *t*'s, sing like you are an Italian," shouted Sam, our former choir director. He didn't get those expressions out of a textbook, but I always understood exactly what he meant. Members of the congregation always praised our choir for our excellent diction. "We understood every word that you sang," was the frequent compliment.

It wasn't until Sam retired that we learned that he had a hearing problem: "word definition," his doctor called it, which meant that he could not hear the beginning and ending consonants unless they were really accentuated. Out of his deficit, our choir became better presenters of God's Holy Word. Isn't that terrific?

Let us pray:

Dear God, take our deficits and turn them into blessings for you as we attempt to spread the gospel of Jesus to every man, woman, and child with whom we come in contact within this congregation, this community, and throughout the whole wide world. Bless us now as we sing. In Jesus' name we pray. Amen.

11 — A Cappella

In the European cathedrals of centuries long since gone, most small chapels had no organ for accompaniment; consequently, the choir sang unaccompanied, or *a cappella*. The style was so beautiful that choirs, even while singing in the larger cathedrals, often sang unaccompanied. Gregorian chant and plainsong were very moving in these large buildings of stone where the acoustics were a marvel to behold. Great composers like Palestrina, Monteverdi, and de Lasso wrote magnificent works in this medium. And much of the great Russian choral music of Tschiakowsky and Rachmaninoff was designed to be sung *a cappella*; the Germans, Brahms, and Schubert, left us a legacy here, too.

Today, most churches with small chapels try to squeeze in an electronic organ or a piano. Synthesizers, drums, and guitars are commonly used in contemporary services. But the style of singing unaccompanied lives on. It is difficult because pitch problems immediately show up. An unsupported tone tends to make a singer flat in pitch. A forced tone with too much edge tends to go sharp. It would be great if every singer went either sharp or flat together, but it usually does not happen that way.

The key to singing in tune is in listening to the singers on each side, the ones in back and in front, and to those other sections across the chancel. As we listen we need to relax the jaw so that all of the tension caused by muscles in the head and neck is gone; then we need to get in touch with the diaphragm. By flexing the diaphragm we allow the air pressure to flow evenly from the lungs, thus allowing the sound literally to float on the air. With this approach, we couldn't sing out of tune even if we wanted to.

Let us pray:

Dear God, we are always aware of your presence as we sing, whether accompanied by organ, piano, a brass choir, or even a full orchestra. Equally so, you are there when we sing *a cappella* or unaccompanied either in the chapel, the sanctuary, or even in the cathedral. Help us to improve our choral singing technique so that our gift of music may be worthy of you. We know that you are always present with us. Bless us as we rehearse this evening. Amen.

12 — Balance

"Sopranos, you're too loud! Tenors, you need to sing out a little more; you have the melody there." Our director, Tom, seemed to be almost obsessed over a balance of parts in our small choir. He even wrote articles for our church paper, pleading for more altos to volunteer for the choir. He never said having a balance was everything, but it surely seemed important to him if you consider how much he talked about it.

According to my confirmation pastor, one should have a balance in all things in life. We all remember the old adage, "All work and no play makes Jack a dull boy!"

When I was a child growing up, my father used to complain about the amount of time my sisters and I spent at the church. On Tuesday afternoon, I accompanied and later conducted the children's choir. Wednesday evening was reserved for Bible study and prayer meeting. And Thursday evening was choir practice. Friday nights were filled by the Sunday school-sponsored roller skating parties and sporting events for the youth. On Sunday, we practically lived at the church: Sunday school and worship in the morning; Epworth League (we were Methodists then) and Sunday evening worship; only to be followed by a Sing at someone's home where we sat in the dark on the living room floor and sang all of the old gospel hymns. To this day I can't remember why we sang in the dark other than we held hands with one or two of the pretty girls sitting near us. Then the boys and girls separated for prayer.

According to my father, we were out of balance. But there was time set aside for school, voice lessons, piano and organ lessons, even conducting lessons and a part-time job. Dates with girls were on Saturday nights, depending on the week's cash flow, and guy things were done on free Friday nights, or in between all of the other week's activities.

How's your life going? Had a vacation lately? Or is your life like the old farmer's wife? Remember the lady who was transported away to the asylum by the men in the white coats? The farmer said to his pastor, "I don't know what's gotten into Mary. She just blew up! Why, she hasn't been out of that kitchen for over thirty years!"

Let us pray:
Dear God, help us to keep a balance in all things of life. Help us to be doers of the Word and not hearers only. May our works for you and our fellow human beings demonstrate our faith. Help us to be mindful of our need for re-creation, time for quiet so that we may hear your still small voice within us. Prepare us now in this rehearsal so that we may sing your praises on Sunday. In Jesus' name we pray. Amen.

13 — Descant

Descant: to discourse on or upon the melody.

A descant always adds color, interest, and beauty to a fine melody. Usually assigned to the first sopranos, this allows some of our finest singers to soar with their high notes with total abandon.

But as my old superintendent used to say, "It's all right to sail your own ship, but please keep it in the fleet!"

Interesting music goes in many directions: counter-melodies, intricate or close harmonies, and fast-changing rhythms. As with all teamwork, this requires every singer to be keenly aware as to what every other section is singing in order to add to the total Gestalt or wholeness of the anthem.

And like a descant, the ministry of music serves as an integral part of our total church program. Because of our visibility in worship services and special services of music, it is so easy to slip into a mode of bringing too much attention to ourselves.

Worship music, if presented well, does not bring undo attention to itself. Rather, it sets moods, it brings life to texts, and it emotionally moves the worshiper to a closer awareness of Almighty God right within his or her very own being.

Let us pray:

Almighty God and Father, use us as instruments to bring those who come to worship to a fuller awareness of you and your Beloved Son, Jesus.

May every aspect of the ministry of music, and specifically this choir, take its place along with the preaching of the Word, the evangelism outreach, the Christian education of children and adults, and all other organizations of this congregation. May all of these efforts serve to bring Jesus and his message of love and grace to every corner of this community. We ask these things in the name of Jesus. Amen.

14 — Mistakes

Remember our director, Sam, who was always so honest? No matter what happened, he always claimed that it was his fault and he took all of the blame. Yes, he made some mistakes, but we didn't ask him if he were perfect when we called him to be our director of music. Besides, can we think of a director who ever demonstrated more love for us?

Well, I remember times when some of us came in a bar too soon or someone hung onto a note too long. It sounded like an impromptu solo. If we want perfection in our services, we should wait for the Heavenly Angels. If we are willing to give of our best, we have the joy of serving Him right here, right now.

Let us pray:

Forgive us for our past and present mistakes, O Heavenly Father, and even for those in our future. For we know that because we are human beings, there will more than likely be other errors, but our very best is all that we have, as imperfect as it may be.

Take our talents and perfect them. Take our dedication to you and to your church and increase and deepen it.

Take our very lives and use them so that the name of Jesus may be lifted up and every knee shall bow. Amen.

15 — Respect

"Respect the composer's wishes," John cried out as he stopped us in the middle of the page. "The marking 'mp' does not stand for 'mighty powerful.' It is more like we would sing a prayer response, medium soft, introspectively or within ourselves, rather than projecting our sound to the back row of the sanctuary like we do when we sing Handel's 'Hallelujah Chorus.' "

We all know that John was probably right with all of those letters after his name. "He's always right," mumbled one of the tenors.

Respect is more important than love. Love can be mushy and sentimental, but respect calls us to action. We show our respect of God as we stand before Him with awe and wonder. But it is the action that demonstrates our commitment. Never listen to the words; watch the feet as they move toward serving Him.

Friends and relatives love us, and because of that love, they never want us to feel any pain. But it is the surgeon who, out of respect for us, puts our very lives at risk as he takes his scalpel and carves away the disease, the cancer.

Maybe that's what God does, too. Out of respect for us, He allows us to go through minor trials and tribulations as a means of making us strong so that we may survive the major pains and problems of this life.

Let us pray:

O God, like Job, we put our trust in you. Help us never to look back, but only forward to see how we may demonstrate our respect, yes, and even our love, as we sing your praises and lead this congregation in worship. In Jesus' name we pray. Amen.

16 — Repertoire

We sing unto the Lord. What does any piece of music in the church do for you personally? Are you moved by the primary children in their Sunday school class as they sing "Jesus Loves Me"? Do you get a tear in your eye during an infant baptism as the congregation sings "Children Of The Heavenly Father"? And on Christmas Eve, with the singing of "Silent Night" by candlelight, what happens to you then? Are these just sentimental moments from which you leave, never to feel anything again? Or does something fine happen to you each time you experience one of these occasions?

And with the music of Johann Sebastian Bach and George Frederick Handel ringing in your ears, what did all of those "Hallelujahs" mean to you, anyway? A chance to improve your florid singing — or a real insight into these men of God — inspiring us to be people of God, too!

I stand in awe and wonder of Bach and Handel because these men allowed Almighty God to speak through them. A mortal man, without inspiration, without waiting upon the Lord to speak through him, could never have written "The Hallelujah Chorus," let alone the entire *Messiah* or the *Mass in B-minor.*

Choir directors select their repertoire from "master composers" whom they feel were "inspired." Surely God was breathing through them. But the repertoire list isn't limited to one set of high musical values; indeed it includes many, so-called lesser composers, too — men and women to whom God spoke, albeit in a very different way than he did to Schubert or Brahms. Directors can't control the writings of the composers, but they can control the selecting.

So, whether the anthem for Sunday is "Sheep May Safely Graze" or "He's Got The Whole World In His Hands," please remember, you are standing on the brink of a tremendous opportunity. An opportunity to get in touch with your many blessings, to feast upon God's love, to feel something so special — your at-oneness with God and your closeness to your fellow man or person, to respond to a text that may redirect your very life, and to influence many, or at least someone, in the congregation toward that more abundant life that Jesus talked about.

I hope that each director is able to find a choral repertoire which brings to him or her personal goose bumps, tears in the eye, and/or lumps in the throat. Then there is a chance that the congregation too will have a right brain experience. Perhaps something very special will move them one step closer to the Throne of Grace.

Let us pray:

Dear God, as we rehearse this evening, help us to improve our diction and our beautiful tone quality so that we may bring to life the texts which we sing — in anthems, hymns, and spiritual songs. May all who come to worship on Sunday have a deeply enriching experience with you and your Son, our dear Lord, Jesus. Amen.

IV. Liturgical Seasons Of The Church Year

December
Date used: _____
By: _____

17 — Advent

The season of Advent includes the four Sundays just before Christmas. This is surely a time to celebrate and to prepare for the coming of the Lord Jesus. Some kin to Palm Sunday, the undertaking invested to pursue this event requires physical stamina and strength for extra and/or lengthy rehearsals, as well as a drain on our musicianship and basic intelligence to learn new and interesting, even if sometimes difficult, music.

All passiveness is gone, for every singer is asked to give of his best to the Master. Inertia or deadness of activity gives way to deep involvement, high commitment, and supreme dedication.

As we seek to greet the Christ Child, the Baby Jesus, anew, our minds and our hearts become more simple, with a fresh, new approach to God's love and His sacrifice for us.

Let us pray:

Dear God, as we prepare for the coming of our Lord, touch our hearts first so that as we sing the story of Jesus' coming it may have special meaning for us which we then communicate to this congregation and all visitors and guests who come to worship in these next few weeks.

May the light of Jesus shine through our smiles, our voices, and the texts and melodies which we sing. May our singing bring all listeners closer to you. And may they become more devoted to walking forevermore in the steps of our Teacher and Friend, Jesus, our Lord. We ask these things in Jesus' name. Amen.

18 — The New Year

In chapters two and three of Colossians, Saint Paul talks about Christ bringing new life to us. As we reflect upon the beginning of a New Year, we have one more opportunity to examine how our lives are going. Rather than making some silly resolutions which we know we will never keep, let us celebrate all that's good in our lives, those characteristics, habits, and lifestyles which we want to carry over into the New Year. Then we can add to, or embellish, what is already right and good for each one of us as followers of Jesus.

Paul writes:

> *You died with Christ. Now the forces of the universe don't have any power over you. Why do you live as if you had to obey such rules as: "Don't handle this. Don't taste that. Don't touch this"? After these things are used, they are no longer good for anything. So why be bothered with the rules that humans have made up? Obeying these rules may seem to be the smart thing to do. They appear to make you love God more and to be very humble and to have control over your body. But they don't really have any power over our desires.*
>
> *You have been raised to life with Christ. Now set your heart on what is in Heaven, where Christ rules at God's right side. Think about what is up there, not about what is here on earth. You died, which means that your life is hidden with Christ, who sits beside God. Christ gives meaning to your life, and when he appears, you will also appear with him in glory.*

Let us pray:

Dear Jesus, we are ready to serve you in Heaven as we have attempted to serve you here on earth. We thank you for leading us safely through this past year, and we ask that you be our Master and our Guide through the year to come. As we read again and again the stories and parables which you told, and the other lessons you taught, may our hearts be always open to receive your message of love; and may our commitment be to take up our cross daily and to follow you. In your name we pray. Amen.

19 — Good Friday

Some time ago, I was mowing my front lawn early one Saturday morning when a young woman from a different religious orientation than mine came to my front door to deliver some tracts and her denomination's monthly magazine. Seeing me going up and down the lawn, she chose to follow me rather than just to drop the material into the mail slot. Being the "gentleman" that I am, I stopped mowing and exchanged pleasantries with her regarding the beautiful spring day and the condition of my pansies which I had just planted.

Then she hit me with, "Sir, do you realize that you are going to hell?" "No, I'm not," I replied vigorously. "Yes, you are," she argued. "You haven't been saved in my church. I was saved on February 6, 1994," she continued, "and I'll never forget it!" "I haven't been saved in anybody's church," I retorted. "I was saved on the original Good Friday when Jesus, the Christ, died for all of us including you and me!"

The young woman gasped, fortunately out of words. I bid her a good morning and continued mowing my front lawn. Since I lived on a corner and there were four directions to go, I didn't see which way she went; she just disappeared. I'm glad that my pastor taught me that way of looking at salvation. I feel so self-assured of my destiny and that of others, especially hers.

Jesus said, "In my Father's house are many mansions." Surely there is a place for this young woman and all other Christians, many of whom feel very strongly about the religious edicts of their particular denomination.

Let us pray:

Dear God, we give you thanks for all believers in Jesus.

Help us to be patient with those religious bodies who arrive at the same heavenly gate by different paths. May we never lose the focus of our eyes being upon you and your beloved Son, Jesus, the Christ. Oft times we share hymns, anthems, and spiritual songs with other denominations. Jointly, may our goal always be to spread the gospel and your love throughout this country and the entire world. In your name we pray. Amen.

20 — Good Friday Revisited

At Christmastime the music is so joyous, lighthearted, happy, and upbeat. It is very hard not to be in a good mood whether shopping at Nieman Marcus, K-Mart, or Sears as we hear the phrase, "Peace on earth, good will toward men."

But the Lenten season is something quite different. After the "Alleluias" of Palm Sunday, we hear Jesus' prayer in the garden, the march to Calvary, and his final words, "Into Thy hands, O Lord, I commend my spirit."

Good Friday has inspired many composers to write about this movingly dramatic event. Publishers' catalogs are loaded with masses, oratorios, cantatas, requiems, and other choral works to set the somber mood for this darkest of religious events.

As singers in the church choir, we can easily get caught up in the emotion of this very sad time in the life of our Savior. But with all of the events of Jesus' life, the birth and the death, we know that our focus must remain on the *Resurrection*. For it is in this event that we find meaning in Jesus' coming to this earth. So the next time we sing about the "Upper Room," or the "Garden of Gethsemane," in the back of our minds we remember too, "Up From The Grave He Arose!" and "Christ Is Risen, Alleluia!" *He is risen indeed!*

Let us pray:

Dear Lord Jesus, we praise your holy name. We stand in awe and wonder at the simplicity of your teachings yet, Lord, sometimes we have difficulty following in your footsteps.

As we sing about your birth, your life and death, and especially about your rising from the dead, help us to open our hearts so that you and the Holy Spirit may dwell within us.

Sing through us, around us, above and beyond us, until that special day when we sing with the holy angels at your Throne of Grace. In your blessed name we pray. Amen.

21 — Easter

Her name was Carolyn and she was our alto soloist/section leader that year. A very funny lady, if a joke could be made of something, Carolyn's sense of humor could be counted upon to set the alto section roaring. And then there was Jim in the tenor section who never wanted to miss a thing. "What did she say? Tell me, what did she say?" he would ask of the other tenors who were trying to pay attention to our director, Don.

Sometimes Carolyn didn't even try to be funny — it just happened that way. I remember the Easter Sunday when the choir was processing to "Jesus Christ Is Risen Today." Because our sanctuary was so small we had to have three services to get everyone in. I guess, because of the sunrise service at 6 a.m. with a rehearsal at 5 a.m. with the brass choir and the handbell choir, we were all a little groggy. Even the relatively strong Swedish coffee (or was it Norwegian?) had only kept us bright-eyed and bushy-tailed through the 8:30 a.m. service. By now, most of us were operating on automatic pilot for this last 10 a.m. service — all except Carolyn.

Our director, Don, had said, "Now remember, ladies and gentlemen, after Susan, our organist, plays the introduction to the hymn, be sure you step out on your left foot. Left foot on the first beat of each bar; right foot on the third beat. Make it appear as though we are a band of Christians flowing into the sanctuary." "Yeah, yeah, we've done this a hundred times. Don't drive it into the ground," said one of the basses. I think it was Sam. He had been a career soldier for more than twenty years.

The sanctuary was so full of worshipers on that Sunday that, at the last minute, the ushers had put folding chairs down both sides of the center aisle. Wow! This was a record crowd. Susan finished the introduction and we began. "Jesus Christ is risen today" — left-right, left-right, and so on. All of us except for Carolyn. Being a little larger and a shorter lady than most of the other altos, she

41

literally filled the narrow space between the two folding chairs. With her hymnal and anthem folder extended as far away from her body as her short arms permitted, she used her lungs and diaphragm to full advantage. Carolyn always sang with gusto, but on Easter Sunday, well, you can imagine how much she put into it — third service and all.

Wearing a big, white Easter hat with about a six-inch brim, one of the parishioners was sitting on a folding chair in the center aisle just in front of Carolyn. The lovely lady bent forward to rise just as Carolyn passed by. You guessed it, the corner of the wide-brimmed Easter bonnet caught on Carolyn's choir folder and hymnal. She had moved up three more aisles before she even became aware that she had the lady's hat still hanging on her music.

All of the singers behind Carolyn tried to hold back their laughter, but to no avail. Susan looked over her music rack from the console trying to see why everyone was laughing instead of singing.

And Jim — remember him in the tenor section — said to Carolyn in the choir room after the service, "You know, when that lady's hat came off it pushed her wig way down over her eyes!" But Don, our director, reminded Carolyn that her solo, "He Shall Feed His Flock" from the *Messiah*, was so beautifully presented that there was not a dry eye in the sanctuary. Indeed, it was a real inspiration.

At any rate, Carolyn did all right for herself, for that same year in June, she married the pastor.

Let us pray:
Dear God, we thank you for the gift of humor. Help us not to take ourselves and others too seriously. Help us rather to focus on the essential reason that we are here: to lead this congregation in worship; to sing your praises with joy; and to give honor to your holy name.

We give you all of the thanks and glory. In Jesus' name we pray. Amen.

V. General Themes

General
Date used: _____
By: _____

22 — Death

Death is a difficult subject about which to sing. There is such a finality to "the end." Musically, composers select dark colors, somber keys, and sad melodic lines to express this mood. Rhythmically, there is seldom a beat, and if there is one, it resembles a funeral dirge. We immediately think of the death of a loved one, or Jesus' death on Good Friday.

But death is not the end. It is only a point of passing on, a transition to new life with God. Every Sunday we celebrate Easter all over again. Jesus rose from the dead. Alleluia!

Some of the most beautiful, emotionally-moving music was written for Holy Week and especially for Good Friday. Many of the world's greatest composers wrote requiems in honor of various departed souls or groups of people.

But thank God, for most of our choral year, we celebrate life: Jesus risen from the tomb. Alleluia! And this celebration allows our faces to light up, our voices to brighten, and our hearts to overflow as we return God's amazing love for us.

Let us pray:

O God, help us not to focus on endings, but on new beginnings. May the rehearsals and services wherein we come together to learn and to serve you, be a whole series of new opportunities to lead your people to the Throne of Grace. And help us not to get so involved in the process of making music that we miss the main event: accepting Jesus as our Lord and Master, and learning from his teachings. For you sent him to be the Savior of the world. In his name we pray. Amen.

23 — Baptism

A few years ago, I was privileged to take a tour through Greece and Turkey titled "The Footsteps of Saint Paul." We visited many of the cities where Paul had preached: Corinth, Ephesus, Thessalonika, and Athens. We even visited the prison where he and Silas sang hymns while they were incarcerated.

One special place I shall always remember was Philippi, the city where the first European, Lydia, was baptized. Within a few feet of the spot, the Greek Orthodox Church had built a new but very small cathedral. No chairs were available and no organ had been installed. Probably the sanctuary could hold only fifty to sixty worshipers — all standing. The stone walls provided beautifully alive acoustics.

My pastor asked me to sing something before we shared a time of prayer. The first piece that came to my mind was the gospel hymn, "Softly And Tenderly," which happened to be my mother's favorite. She would have loved to have had someone sing this at her funeral, but my father insisted on a graveside burial without music. He felt music made those attending the funeral feel very sad.

Before I sang, I explained this to our small travel group, and several of the women did cry softly as I sang the words, "Come home, come home. Ye who are weary, come home!" Later I learned that one had just lost her mother and another expected her mother to die at any time.

The recollection of the Baptismal Place of Lydia and that little Greek Orthodox Cathedral shall remain with me always.

Let us pray:

Dear God, as we sing the gospel hymns of an earlier time, touch our heart strings so that we may make a full contact with Jesus, our Lord, his teachings, and his love.

Bless us now as we participate in this choir. Help us to sing beautifully for you. In Jesus' name we pray. Amen.

44

24 — The Baptismal Font

Pastor John was our new intern for that year. On his first Sunday, he really wanted to make a good first impression. Rather than giving the announcements from the lectern as our senior pastor always did, he chose to walk right down the center aisle so that he could speak directly to the people. Since, like in most churches, no one was sitting in the first five rows, this required Pastor John to pass the baptismal font and to speak about ten feet in front of it.

Earlier that morning, the altar committee moved the font to the center of the aisle and filled it with warm water for the baptism which was to be held later in the service. As the announcements finished, you guessed it, Pastor John started backing up, completely forgetting that the baptismal font was there. Just as he was announcing the opening hymn, he fell over the baptismal font, completely knocking it down. The water went in one direction and Pastor John went in the other. His robe flew through the air and all one could see of this very embarrassed young man as he hit the floor were the soles of his shoes. Indeed, he had made a very lasting first impression on our congregation.

Let us pray:

Lord, as we try so hard to do our very best, help us to keep our sense of humor. Yes, we feel bad when we enter a beat too early, or if we sing wrong notes, but we realize that you are not judging our gift. Rather, you welcome the best that we have. And in those services when our best is not perfect, we don't allow ourselves to feel bad, because you have promised us grace and forgiveness. Help us to continue to love ourselves because you first loved us — and that makes us lovable. We return that love to you and to your dear Son, Jesus, the Christ, through our commitment and dedication to this service of love as we sing with joy in our hearts. Bless our rehearsal this evening and bring us back on Sunday to sing your praises. Amen.

25 — Compassion

Is compassion really in the Duty Statement of a singer in this choir?

The Good Samaritan bound up the beaten man's wounds. Jesus washed the disciples' feet; then there was the woman who poured the expensive oil on Jesus's head.

Some churches provide food for the homeless while others sponsor child care for single parents who are very poor. I guess that there are a lot of ways in which we can demonstrate compassion either as an individual or as a congregation. How should we be showing our compassion to others?

Let us pray:

Dear God, help each one of us to look deeply into ourselves to see how we can show compassion to our fellow men, women, and children.

Help us not to get so caught up in the joy of serving you in this congregation that we forget about serving others in the larger community — especially those who are unchurched. We are reminded of Jesus' words, "If you have done it unto the least of these my brethren, you have done it unto me."

As a new week awaits us, help us to be ever searching for people who need you. Let us be the mediums through which you touch another human being. We are so happy to be yours, help us to bring others to your Throne of Grace. If it takes a word, a smile, the touch of a hand, encourage us to take a risk, to win someone for you, O Heavenly Father. Amen.

26 — Director

As a member of the Worship Committee, I was asked recently to represent our congregation at a church music conference. When the chairperson asked me to go, I laughed right out loud. "What do I know about church music?" I asked. "I've only been singing in church choirs for forty years." Not heeding my attempt to beg off, and being a strong chairperson, I was summarily given the directions, "Take good notes!"

The conference started the very next day. After the morning session, I sat down at the luncheon table with several other attendees from neighboring churches. I bragged just a little about Linda, our new choir director. "She's really great," I said to the group.

Sitting next to me was a sweet little lady, beautifully dressed and tastefully groomed. "Are you the director of your choir?" I asked. "Heavens, no!" she replied. "I'm only the pastor's wife." "Is your director here?" I continued. "Oh, yes," she said. "You see, God directs our choir. I just select the music and tell the singers when to stand up and when to sit down. Each singer is responsible for learning well his or her own music, because he or she knows that God expects it to be perfect." "Who sets the tempo and tells the group when to begin and when to stop?" I asked. "Oh, I do that, but we all know that God is really our director."

Let us pray:

Dear God, we acknowledge you to be the leader, the director, in all things. You preach through our pastor, you sing through us, and you reach out to this community through every member and friend of this congregation.

Help us to be ever mindful, and so totally inspired by your great love for us, that we may constantly tell the story of Jesus to all who will listen. May our lives be a testimony to your love working within each one of us. Amen.

27 — I Am Nothing

One of the pastors with whom I had the privilege of serving for many years used to tell a story which I believe he had read in an old issue of *Reader's Digest*. It went something like this.

An artist looked out of his windows each day for inspiration for his next painting. For several days in a row a homeless man passed while pushing a grocery cart which contained all of his belongings. On one particular day, the artist went out to the street as the man was approaching. He asked him for permission to paint him. The man was only too happy to earn a few dollars and, without fail, daily he showed up for each sitting. When he asked to see the painting, the artist put him off until it was finished.

Finally, on that fateful day of completion, the artist allowed the old man to see the finished work. He was amazed that the artist had captured every detail in his timeworn face. But he was alarmed when he saw that his hair had been cut, his beard trimmed, and that he was dressed in a beautiful suit.

"Who is that?" asked the old man. "Why, it is you," responded the artist. "Don't you like it?" "Oh, yes," said the man. "If it is possible for me to be like that, I will be it!"

Let us pray:

Dear God, give us each a vision as to what we can become as your children — not only as singers in this choir, but in every area of our lives.

Help us to reach out in love to others to put our faith into works. There are so many needy in this world. Put us in touch with those who are in want of food and clothing, especially those who need our listening ear and our compassion. Speak through us when we don't know what to say. May all that we do and say lead others to our Lord Jesus, the Christ. We dedicate our voices now to proclaim your Holy Name. Amen.

28 — The Last Song

Somewhere back in the 1940s, film star Jeanette MacDonald was featured on a radio drama. Remember radio? That was before television. In the drama, Miss MacDonald played the part of a very famous opera singer who was in need of surgery on her throat in order to save her life. Her throat specialist was also her husband. The part of the surgeon was played by Gene Raymond, who in real life was her husband.

Following the surgery, it was anticipated that she would never sing again. Without the surgery, death was imminent. For most of the one-half hour drama, the couple spend time together in a row boat on a lake. Dr. Raymond rows and Miss MacDonald sings to him for her last time. Perhaps the selection was her favorite aria, or their very special love song. At any rate, it was very romantic.

All of us take for granted the beautiful voices which God has bestowed upon us. Our singing over the years has brought personal pleasure to us and joy to our many listeners. As we contemplate all of the rich blessings which Almighty God has bestowed upon us, let us pause for a moment now and thank Him.

Let us pray:

O Lord, our Heavenly Father, we set aside these brief moments this evening to thank you for all of the goodness that you have given to each one of us in this choir. We are especially grateful for our voices which allow us to sing your praises. We too are mindful of the gift of hearing so that we may sing in harmony with others and the gift of sight so that we may read your Word and learn the sacred choral music of the ages. In deepest love, O Lord, Sunday by Sunday we return these gifts to you as we worship before your very Throne of Grace. Bless us now as we rehearse this evening. Amen.

29 — Maturity

Under the best of circumstances, birth is a traumatic experience. Unless there were unusual complications, most of us survived the experience quite well.

And then through childhood and the teenage years, we grew. We became educated. We experienced life in all of its fullness. Does anyone here wish to live through the teenage years a second time?

Scientists tell us that we reached our prime in the late twenties, someplace between 26 and 28 years of age. From then on, it has been downhill all of the way. The tenors and basses have watched their muscles atrophy and fall off, their abdomens sag, and in some cases, even their hair starting to fall out. Sopranos and altos have experienced changes too, but we won't relate those this evening. This is a cycle.

This perception sounds very negative. The positive outlook reminds us of our greater maturity, wisdom, and graciousness. These are qualities to be revered as the years go by.

Vocally, for those of us in this church choir, our voices have taken on a depth and richness which we didn't have when we were young. We now sing with compassion and meaning because we have experienced life in its sadness as well as in its joy. And we now appreciate very highly the gift of music which we bring to our Sunday worshipers and to God and His Son, Jesus.

Let us pray:
Dear God, we thank you for the privilege of serving you for many years in your kingdom here on earth. Bless us now to continue our commitment and dedication for whatever time we have left on this earth. Because of Jesus, our Lord, and him crucified, we are always ready to join the Heavenly Choir to sing with the angels your praises for all eternity. May our faces shine with radiance as we sing for you, this rehearsal, and for each Lord's Day. We pray in the name of Jesus. Amen.

30 — Museum Piece

I don't know who selects the music for this choir, but sometimes I really wonder about it. I know the pastor picks the hymns, and by the end of the service I can usually see how the texts all tie in together with his sermon theme. Sometimes he slips in an old gospel hymn like "Amazing Grace" which always makes me teary-eyed because it was used at my friend's funeral. At other times, we practically dance to something more contemporary like "Soon And Very Soon," one of those songs in our new hymnal.

I guess John, our new choir director, picks the music for the choir. I like it when the anthem has a good melody and beautiful harmonies. Occasionally though, he passes one out that has a "rip-snorting" beat. Then he adds guitars and drums, and our organist moves over to the synthesizer. Do you remember that Sunday when he asked us to do a two-step to that African piece? It was fun. I wanted to leave the choir loft and dance right down the center aisle while waving my arms. At lunch that day, I shared this idea with my family. Boy, were they glad that I didn't do that. My fourteen-year-old daughter said that she would have been so embarrassed that she would have never been able to show her face in this congregation again. I didn't think my idea was that bad. All of the above are great with me. I really like the variety.

Every once in a while, John gives this "lecture" on the importance of singing very early music. When, in his opinion, the English translation is not very good, we try the Latin. "I haven't had Latin since high school back in the '40s," I said. "All I remember is alpha and omega, something about the beginning and the end." Then that smart-alec tenor, Jim, opened his big mouth and said, "Are you sure it wasn't in the '30s?" Humph! What does he know. I was out of college before he was born.

Well, we learned our Latin. It took a little time and a lot of concentration, but we did it. During the coffee hour after the Sunday service at which we presented this anthem, one of the ushers said to me, "Hey, how come you guys were singing in Latin today? Wasn't that what the Reformation was all about — to sing hymns in our native tongue?"

This upset me so that I called the pastor on Monday morning. When I explained my problem, he said, "You know, Latin is kind of like a universal language. Even Johann Sebastian Bach, who was one of the greatest of Lutheran musicians who ever lived, chose to set certain choral works to Latin texts. They can be quite inspiring and the words are easily translatable. But your usher friend may have a point. Some pieces are perhaps better presented at special services when the entire program is music and those who really feel inspired by these great works can have a wonderful thrill for the whole Sunday afternoon. But like you, I'm not sure that they are always appropriate for Sunday morning worship services."

"Yes," I said, "but what about those who have a very limited musical and spiritual background? Can they receive anything from this trip to the museum?" And pastor said, "Isn't that why we established our contemporary service?"

Let us pray:

Dear God, you speak through the immortal giants of music: Bach, Handel, Mozart, and Mendelssohn. And you speak just as clearly through some of our more recent composers: Amy Grant, Tom Fettke, Andre Crouch, John Ness Beck, and Craig Courtney. All of the people who come to worship in our sanctuary represent different cultures and backgrounds, different religious experiences, and certainly different educations — especially musical educations.

But we are one in the same in our search for you and your dear Son, Jesus, our Lord. Since our backgrounds are so diversified, help us to balance out the formal with the informal, the high church liturgy with the low church more simple service of praise. May all who come to this hallowed place of worship, fall on their knees in deepest humility, but rise through your grace and forgiveness to go out into this community to spread the gospel of Jesus to the lost, the downtrodden, the faint, and those who have made mistakes in their lives.

Take us; use us to your honor and glory. We give you all of the praise as we sing our unending thanks. Amen.

General
Date used: _____
By: _____

31 — Spirituality

In many of the devotions in this booklet, the author has attempted to get to the real heart of the meaning of various words to make worship more meaningful — more alive for both singers in the choir loft and worshipers in the pew.

The death of choral music in the worship service comes when it can be described as dull or apathetic, presented by singers who are indifferent and/or unconcerned.

To bring spirituality to music in worship requires more than just singing religious or sacred words, but in setting a lively and vigorous mood which breathes life and enthusiasm into the text — not so much focusing on the literal words, but more on the spirit of the message, the soul of what the composer intended to present. And this does not mean that any anthem should be fast, but rather sung with an aliveness of tone and an expression on each singer's face which says, "I believe."

With boldness, courage, and vivaciousness, the intent is to move the worshiper from complacency or from being an observer or listener, to feeling something so moving that he or she will become totally involved. The worshiper can catch a vision as to what he or she can do to become a part of God's plan to spread the word of Jesus — about his teachings, his death and resurrection — and about the story of the Savior of the world.

Spirituality? Yes! God breathing through us the essence or the substance of who He is in relation to who we are — with the Lord Jesus leading us every step of the way as we seek to serve him daily, especially by our singing, but within, around, and through everything we do and say every day of our lives.

Let us pray:
Dear God, we want to be effective in our service. So right now, help us just to release and let go as we turn our lives over to you.

Take our voices, our thoughts, and even our physical energy and channel them into your design for spreading to every corner of this world the Word about Jesus. As we start right here in this congregation and within this community, may all that we do and say be done for your honor and glory. Amen.

General

Date used: _____

By: _____

32 — On Time

As a high school student, I was always late. If a meeting was scheduled to begin at 7:30 p.m., you could count on my never being there on time. Usually at 7:30 p.m. I was still standing in my bedroom and it was a five-minute drive to the church, or a ten-minute walk. With gas rationing (remember World War II?), I usually walked.

One evening, as usual, I was late for the adult choir practice. When I arrived, the choir was part way through sight reading "The Heavens Are Telling" from Haydn's *The Creation*. For those of you who have never sung this piece, the vocal lines are "contrapuntal," which means that everybody sings the melody but at different times. The entrances are tricky and even good musicians find it necessary to count.

Just as I took my place in the choir loft, the whole choir broke down and roared at their poor sight-reading skills. The organist gave fresh pitches and they were off and running again. One of the tenors quickly told me the page that they were on, but not the place on the page. I began singing, holding my part very well, or so I thought — until I reached the end of the last page. Since I had run out of notes, I stopped. All of the other tenors had stopped too, because they were totally lost — which is not uncommon for tenors.

I flipped back a few pages quickly trying to find where the basses were singing. Once again I sang to the end and the sopranos and altos kept right on going. By now, the basses were totally lost too. And again, I flipped back a few pages to find the soprano part and when I got to the end this time, lo and behold, we all finished together.

"How did all of you do?" asked Marian, our choir director. There were giggles and amusing comments from many. Then the director, assuming me to be a good sight reader, asked me, "Fred, you seemed to finish with the rest of us. How did you get along?"

"I'm not quite sure," I replied, "but I had to sing the last page three times." The choir laughed at my honesty. "Serves you right," said Marian. "Next time you'll get here on time and start with the rest of us." I was very embarrassed and probably red-faced. But I was never late again to that choir's rehearsals.

Can a person be late in coming to Jesus? Isn't it true that God has been with us since our births? In some cases, some persons just don't know that He has been waiting for them to turn to Him. It is never too late to commit to following Jesus. For as we follow in his footsteps, we will bring others to the Father.

Let us pray:
Dear God, as we reach out for the unchurched, those who seem not to know you, help us not to forget those who may be a little older. For it is never too late to come into your House of Prayer, your Tabernacle, your Very Presence. Give us inner peace this evening as we serve you in this choir. Then tomorrow and all the days of our lives, we will step out as missionaries for you, ministering to those who have never heard the wondrous story of your love. In the name of Jesus, we pray. Amen.

33 — Overalls

It was in the middle of the Depression, about 1932, when the young pastor and his bride of two weeks arrived at the little country church. Pastor Allen had just finished the seminary and this was his very first call. The choir was very short of singers so he decided to call on all of the former members to find out why they had dropped out of the choir. Was the director too demanding, did he yell at the bass section when they came in a bar too early, did he embarrass the tenor section in some way? Why were these singers no longer coming to church to sing God's praises?

It all came to light when he stopped by Harold's farm. This was a man who had won the high school state championship for his playing of the trumpet. And in college, he had organized a male quartet which traveled each summer all over the United States. The programs which the quartet gave in local churches provided for their tuition the next year.

"Tell me, Harold," said Pastor Allen, "I've noticed that you and your family haven't attended services for most of this past year. And according to Ben, our choir director, you were the best bass the choir had." "Well, Pastor, you see, it is like this. I'm not mad at anybody. I just can't afford nice clothes anymore. I had to give my oldest son my only suit. He's growing like a weed. I can't afford a new suit, so I can't come to church to sing anymore." "Not so," said the pastor. "Let's make a deal. Come next Sunday. I'm going to wear a pair of overalls just like yours. And I'm going to wear them every Sunday until the economy changes in this community and we can all afford to buy new suits. Is it a deal?"

"Yes," said Harold. "It is a deal!" And for the next eighteen months, Pastor Allen, who also sang in the choir, and Harold stood side by side singing the Lord's praises in that little church choir. And as the anthem finished each Sunday, the two men would look at each other and smile. It was as though they were saying in unison, "God doesn't care what we wear! He just wants us to sing like His angels!"

Let us pray:

Take away our need to be overly formal, O Lord. Rather, let us focus on the main reason we are here: to proclaim you as God the Almighty, the Ruler of the universe, and to honor your dear Son, our beloved Lord Jesus. As we follow in his footsteps, help us to make it possible for all men and women, boys and girls, the poor and the wealthy, the depressed and the downtrodden, and those exhilarating with joy — for all of us to come before you with singing. Amen.

34 — Personality

Every choir has a unique sound or personality. Sometimes it is easily identified through the size of the ensemble, the choral tone, or even its deportment as with professional ensembles who choreograph their concerts on a stage. Local church choirs often are noted for their emphasis on repertoire: early Gregorian chants; the classics of Bach and Handel; the more current, almost "pop" style of strong rhythms, predictable harmonies, and easily learned repetitious melodies. And then there's the whole contemporary scene, kind of a modern folk song approach with three or four chords, using two or more guitars.

It is fun to hear a choral sound change as soon as a new conductor steps to the podium. I recall festivals over the years wherein combined choirs of 100 to 200 singers sang a repertoire of six or so anthems — each with a different conductor. As each new conductor stepped to the podium, already the thinking of each singer was readjusting: rounder vowel sounds for one conductor for a lovelier tone; more distinct consonants for another for clarity of text; and perhaps cleaner entrances and very precise cutoffs for yet another.

Even the playing of the magnificent, world renowned Los Angeles Philharmonic Orchestra changed from Alfred Wallenstein's beautiful *pianissimos* in Mozart; to Eduard van Beinum's stirring rhythms in Tschiakowsky; to Zubin Mehta's soaring melodies of Richard Strauss and breathtaking melodic lines of Gustav Mahler; to the poet Carlo Maria Giulini's wonderful phrasing of Brahms and Beethoven; to Andre Previn's famous French interpretations; to Esa-Pekka Salonen's inspiring readings of the most modern day composers. Each conductor requested and got an entirely different sound, and in his own way, made beautiful music.

Glen Miller, the great dance bandleader of the '30s and '40s, spent a lifetime looking for a special sound that he heard in his head and attempted to recreate through his orchestrations.

And what about this choir? Those of you who have sung in this same choir for many years probably remember how your choral sound has changed from conductor to conductor. But with each new musician who approaches your podium, the focus has been not only to make a beautiful choral sound, but to come into His presence with singing, to give thanks to the Lord, for He is good, to make a joyful noise unto the Lord, to sing to the Lord a new song, to sing to the Lord, all the earth — bless His name, to serve the Lord with gladness, to tell of His salvation from day to day, and declare His glory among the nations.

The Lord reigns! His steadfast love endures forever!

Let us pray:

O God, no matter how beautifully we sing from a technical point of view, may we never lose sight of our main purpose for being here in this choir. Let the beauty of Jesus be seen in us individually and as a choir. May our anthems inspire our worshipers to a closer walk with you. In spite of our fun together, or perhaps even because of it, may the fellowship we experience here this evening spill over to every member of this blessed congregation. With deep love for you, O Heavenly Father, we sing to spread the gospel of Jesus and him crucified. Amen.

35 — Pride

We were really great last Sunday! Boy, that anthem really wowed 'em! Those sopranos marched up to those high notes and belted them out with such ease — just like Kirsten Flagstad, or was it Ethel Merman! And those tenors, why, they sounded like the whole cello section right out of the Philharmonic Orchestra.

"But wait a minute," Dave, our director, said. "It was okay to feel good about our successes, but remember, it is God who sings through us. We want God to speak to every worshiper at our services. For some this may happen as they gaze at the stained-glass windows. For others it may be in hearing the majesty of our organ. Yet for still others, it might happen through the smile and the handshake of that little old lady who greets people at the front door each Sunday."

I guess Dave was trying to tell us that our music, no matter how perfect, is there just to lead men, women, and children to the Throne of Grace. It feels terrific, but we should be giving all of the glory and honor to Him.

Let us pray:

Dear God, help us never to forget that we are your children. You created us in your spiritual image. And, as such, we have a great deal to feel good about. We thank you for giving us the talent to sing your praises so well.

But, Lord, keep us humble too. Take away all false pride and help us focus on your Son, Jesus, our Lord. May we follow in his footsteps, this day and always. Amen.

36 — Sea Of Galilee

Several years ago, I had the privilege of visiting the Holy Lands with my pastor and others from our congregation. Communion was served in a garden in front of the tomb where Jesus was supposedly buried. We visited Bethlehem, the very spot where Mary was said to have given birth to the baby Jesus. But the most memorable experience for me, of all of the places we visited, was the Sea of Galilee. The motor boat which took us from Tiberius to Capernaum was very quiet. No one aboard spoke and many eyes were filled with tears — reflecting the emotion of the moment. The sea was as smooth as glass, with not even a ripple in the water.

As we left our vessel on the other side, we soon approached the spot where Jesus is said to have given "The Sermon on the Mount." What hallowed ground — the spot where our Lord had come down from the mountain. It reminded me so of the old solo, "I Walked Today Where Jesus Walked."

Let us pray:

Dear Jesus, may we always walk in your footsteps. Teach us the right thing to do in all situations. And when in doubt, help us to close our mouths and to open our ears, our minds, and especially our hearts to that still small voice within us that guides us to life everlasting. In your name we pray. Amen.

37 — The Wedding

For many years, Pastor Bill had been the senior pastor of his church in a rather large city in one of the middle states. He was considered to be the religious leader for the whole city because he was looked up to by pastors and priests of many different religious bodies. If you tried to think of someone who was very dignified, who moved with grace and composure, first and foremost, Pastor Bill always came to mind.

When he preached or read the scripture, his smooth, silvery-throated voice was a mixture of Orson Welles, Laurence Olivier, and Richard Burton. If he had been a classic actor, easily he could have won an academy award.

One Sunday morning in August, the air-conditioning system failed in Pastor Bill's church and the sanctuary was more than 100 degrees in temperature. The gentlemen in the congregation removed their coats and loosened their neck ties and every lady in the sanctuary made a fan out of her church bulletin. The fanning only made them hotter, but they fanned away just the same.

During the second hymn, up in the choir loft one rather large soprano was overcome by the heat and was carried by several tenors — remember them, the ones with the muscles? They have never been the same. After that, the whole alto section unzipped their robes and threw them back. Truly, this was a hot Sunday. Pastor Bill even mentioned that this would have been a great Sunday to preach about hell.

The daughter of the president of the congregation was to be married that same Sunday at 2:30 p.m. Her father, not wanting anyone to pass out during the ceremony, especially the bride or groom, unbeknown to Pastor Bill, rented several large fans which he placed in the chancel close to the altar. If not cooler, at least the air would circulate.

Meanwhile, Pastor Bill, who that morning had come close to heat prostration himself, decided to wear for the wedding only his underwear under his long black robe. The robe was so long that only his black shoes and a little of his black socks would probably show anyway. Or so it seemed.

All of the rented fans were aimed at the railing where the bride and groom would be kneeling. As Pastor Bill entered the chancel area, he experienced quite a rustling of his robe. As he took his place in front of the altar, all of the fans attacked him at once. His robe flew up to his hips — a perfect advertisement for the Jockey Company.

Obviously, the sedate congregation which had assembled for the ceremony went into wild hysterics. The ladies blushed and the men from Pastor Bill's softball team exchanged comments which we can't print here. Old Ms. Jones had to be taken out for some water. After the fans were turned off and the wedding party regained its composure, the wedding went off without a hitch.

Later that week, the society editor for the local newspaper wrote an article for her column. In describing the wedding, she mentioned the beauty of the bride and the lovely dresses worn by the bridesmaids. She closed her article with, "And, folks, this was certainly the most 'eventful' wedding that I have ever attended in this city. I'm still laughing every time that I think about Pastor Bill's knees. They were so cute!"

Let us pray:

Thank you, Heavenly Father, for bringing us back to reality once in a while. No matter how highly exalted we feel that we may be, you remind us from time to time of our need to be humble.

We thank you for a sense of humor that helps us to laugh at ourselves. But we count it a privilege, too, to be serving with a wonderful pastor in his efforts to reach out to this community. We ask your special blessing on him and for his success in ministering among us.

As a real team for Jesus, help us to keep a light touch as we work hard together to spread the gospel. May our music, which is dedicated to you, please you. Accept it as our gift of love. In Jesus' name we pray. Amen.

General
Date used: _____
By: _____

38 — Sanctuary

When I was a child, I was taught not to speak loudly in the sanctuary, certainly not to run or play there, and usually not even to laugh, unless of course our pastor told a joke. But even that was rare. In Sunday school we learned about the prophets of old who built altars to God. So then the altar and the communion table were very significant too. We were instructed never to go behind the communion rail.

As an adult, one Sunday morning between services, I was cleaning up old bulletins and rearranging the hymnals and Bibles in the pew racks. Suddenly, when I looked up, here were too little boys down in the organ pit, one crawling on the pedal board and the other pulling very hard on the draw knobs of our new console. I was horrified. I spoke to the boys, in not too kindly a tone of voice, and ordered them to get away from the organ console. They ran, but only to continue their play behind the communion rail. They were laughing and apparently having great fun.

Just as I reached the altar, one had the offering plates in hand and the other was pulling on the white linen altar cloth. Just in time, I caught the trays with the communion glasses. Taking each boy by the hand, I sat them down in the front pew with the instructions, "Don't you move until your mother comes." As soon as I looked away, they were gone.

Moments later, their mother came down the aisle literally fuming. "What do you mean by upsetting my boys?" she asked. "You can see that they are only little children. They were just playing!"

Where do we draw the line between teaching our children to respect the sanctuary and its most holy of holies, the altar — and helping them to feel welcome so that they will return again?

65

Let us pray:

Dear God, give us patience in dealing with others, especially little children. We walk into your tabernacle with a sense of awe and wonder. In addition to your presence in a building made of stone, wood, and glass, help us to focus on your dwelling within our hearts whether we be in the solitude of our small bedrooms at home, or in the open spaces of your great mountains, majestic green trees, and cold streams. We love you as we know you love us. Bless us as we rehearse this evening so that we may be ready to fill your sanctuary with gorgeous music, dedicated to you. Amen.

VI. Closing Of The Choir Season

May

Date used: _____

By: _____

39 — Duets, Trios, And Quartets

"Oh, I can't sing a solo," I said to Alice, our choir director, as she was setting up the special summer music schedule. She canvasses all of the singers each spring because our choir doesn't sing after Memorial Day weekend. I really enjoy singing in the choir and I miss it all summer when we sit in the pews. Thursday evenings are very special to me because I have a lot of problems at home and it gives me a chance to forget about them as I sing for the Lord. I probably shouldn't admit it, but I like to come early and stay late so that I have lots of time to visit with my friend, Jane.

Jane and I have been singing together for twenty years and we hold down the second soprano section against all of those really loud first sopranos. I can tell Jane anything and she always responds with, "I'll be praying for you." Then usually on a Monday or a Tuesday, I get a brief telephone call from her, just checking to see how I'm doing. And when she misses a rehearsal or a Sunday, I always call her to see if she's well or needs something.

When Jane and I whisper during a rehearsal, Alice always gives me "the look" and I become very silent, usually in the middle of a sentence.

"No, Alice," I said, "I can't do a solo, but why don't you put me down for a trio?" "Great," said Alice. "How about July 15? You'll get a lot of encouragement from the other two singers." Little did she know that Jane has been encouraging me for twenty years. Many times when I was ready to leave the church, I hung in there because Jane never allowed me to feel alone. My singing in this choir for all of these years and my first trio may be an inspiration for members of the congregation and others who come to worship on Sunday, but it is Almighty God who has encouraged and inspired me through my good friend, Jane, and she doesn't even know it. I hope we can sing together for another twenty years. By the way, the trio went well. Next year, I'm signing up for a duet with Jane. And the year after that, well, we'll see.

Let us pray:

Dear God, thank you for every member of this choir. And thank you, too, for using us in ways in which we may not even be aware. Help us to reach out for others even when we think they may be all right. Help us never to assume anything, either good or bad, but to let you work through us to help others in need. Help us to be doers of your Word, for we ask it in Jesus' name. Amen.

40 — Choir Recognition

I always enjoy our choir recognition service at the end of the choir season. The competition for the attendance award is just simple fun. We all try to attend every rehearsal and service, but you know how it goes. Illness, travel, out of town guests, and sometimes we are just too tired to go out one more night, even for the Lord.

But our congregation smiles so much that I know they really appreciate our efforts. Sometimes when we sing, there isn't a dry eye in the sanctuary. For not only is the congregation deeply moved, but so are we. I remember one Sunday, when the tears were overflowing even from the eyes of Jack, our director.

Yet there are other Sundays when our anthem sets the toes to tapping, we end in a big glorious sound and, spontaneously, the congregation breaks into applause. I was always taught that applause was not appropriate in church. If you liked something, you just shouted, "Amen!" But why not applaud? Sometimes I feel that God is smiling down on this choir and He must be saying, "Well done, my good and faithful servants!"

Let us pray:

Our loving Heavenly Father, we want so much to please you, to continue to serve you well. We thank you for giving each of us a voice, good health, and a sense of humor. Help us to take time to rest and relax this summer. And as we become refreshed, bring us back safely in the fall so that we may continue to sing your praises. As always, we give you the honor and the glory. Amen.

VII. Closing Devotions

Date used: _____
By: _____

1 — September

Numbers 6:22-27

The Lord told Moses,
"When Aaron and his sons bless the people of Israel, they must
    say:

I pray that the Lord will bless and protect you,
And that he will show you mercy and kindness.
May the Lord be good to you and give you peace."

Then the Lord said, "If Aaron and his sons ask me to bless the
    Israelites, I will give them my blessing." Amen.

Date used: _____
By: _____

2 — October

2 Thessalonians 3:16, 18

I pray that the Lord, who gives you peace, will always bless
    you with peace.
May the Lord be with all of you.

I pray that our Lord Jesus Christ will be kind to all of you.
    Amen.

3 — November

1 Kings 8:54-61

When Solomon finished his prayer at the altar, he was kneeling with his arms lifted toward heaven.
He stood up, turned toward the people, blessed them, and said loudly:

Praise the Lord!
He has kept his promise and given us peace.
Every good thing he promised to his servant Moses has happened.

The Lord our God was with our ancestors to help them, and I pray that he will be with us and never abandon us.
May the Lord help us obey him and follow all the laws and teachings he gave our ancestors.

I pray that the Lord our God will remember my prayer day and night.
May he help everyone in Israel each day, in whatever way we need it.
Then every nation will know that the Lord is the only true God.

Obey the Lord our God and follow his commands with all your heart just as you are doing today. Amen.

4 — December

Romans 15:5-6, 13

God is the one who makes us patient and cheerful.
I pray that he will help you live at peace with each other, as
you follow Christ.
Then all of you together will praise God, the Father of our
Lord Jesus Christ.

I pray that God, who gives hope, will bless you with complete
happiness and peace because of your faith.
And may the power of the Holy Spirit fill you with hope. Amen.

Date used: _____
By: _____

5 — January

Romans 16:25-27

Praise God!
He can make you strong by means of my good news, which is
the message about Jesus Christ.
For ages and ages this message was kept secret, but now at last
it has been told.
The eternal God commanded His prophets to write about the
good news, so that all nations would obey and have faith.

And now, because of Jesus Christ, we can praise the only wise
God forever! Amen.

Date used: _____
By: _____

6 — February

2 Corinthians 13:11-13

Good-bye, my friends. Try to get along and live peacefully with each other.

Now I pray that God, who gives love and peace, will be with you.
Give each other a warm greeting.
All of God's people send their greetings.

I pray that the Lord Jesus Christ will bless you and be kind to you!
May God bless you with His love, and may the Holy Spirit join all your hearts together. Amen.

Date used: _____
By: _____

7 — March

Ephesians 6:23-24

I pray that God the Father and the Lord Jesus Christ will give peace, love, and faith to every follower!

May God be kind to everyone who keeps on loving our Lord Jesus Christ. Amen.

8 — April

Philippians 4:4-9

Always be glad because of the Lord!
I will say it again; Be glad.
Always be gentle with others.
The Lord will soon be here.
Don't worry about anything, but pray about everything.
With thankful hearts offer up your prayers and requests to God.

Then, because you belong to Christ Jesus, God will bless you
    with peace that no one can completely understand.
And this peace will control the way you think and feel.

Finally, my friends, keep your minds on whatever is true, pure,
    right, holy, friendly, and proper.
Don't ever stop thinking about what is truly worthwhile and
    worthy of praise.
You know the teachings I gave you, and you know what you
    heard me say and saw me do.
So follow my example.
And God, who gives peace, will be with you. Amen.

9 — May

Hebrews 13:20-21

God gives peace, and He raised our Lord Jesus Christ from death.
Now Jesus is like a Good Shepherd whose blood was used to make God's eternal agreement with his flock.

I pray that God will make you ready to obey Him and that you will always be eager to do right.
May Jesus help you do what pleases God.
To Jesus Christ be glory forever and ever! Amen.

Date used: _____
By: _____

10 — June

Jude 24-25

Offer praise to God our Savior because of our Lord Jesus Christ!
Only God can keep you from falling and make you pure and
joyful in His glorious presence.
Before time began and now and forevermore, God is worthy
of glory, honor, power, and authority. Amen.

The Lord's Prayer
Matthew 6:9-13

Our Father in heaven, help us to honor your name.
Come and set up your kingdom, so that everyone on earth will
obey you, as you are obeyed in heaven.
Give us our food for today.
Forgive us for doing wrong, as we forgive others.
Keep us from being tempted and protect us from evil. Amen.

Matthew 6:9-13 (KJV)

Our Father which art in heaven, Hallowed be thy name.
Thy kingdom come,
Thy will be done in earth, as it is in heaven.

Give us this day our daily bread.
And forgive us our trespasses, as we forgive those who tres-
pass against us.
And lead us not into temptation, but deliver us from evil:
For thine is the kingdom, and the power, and the glory, forever
and ever. Amen.

77

VIII. Orders Of Worship

The Service Of Choir Dedication

(The Pastor invites the Choir to join him at the altar.)

Pastor: O loyal friends of Jesus, why have you come before the altar this morning?

Choir: **We wish to dedicate our service to the Lord, our God.**

Pastor: How do you wish to serve Him?

Choir: **With our voices in melody, harmony, and rhythm. We want to sing His praises all the day long, but especially at the time of worship of this congregation.**

Pastor: But won't that take a commitment of your time, your talent, and your love?

Choir: **We are ready, Pastor. God has given us these voices with which to sing His praises. We simply want to return to Him the gifts that He has first given us. Now and always, may all that we do here musically, in these services of worship, serve only to glorify His name. By our dedicated service each week, may we express our love and devotion to Him. We are honored to know that He sings through us. He uses us as vessels to reach the hearts of those who come to worship, Sunday by Sunday.**

Pastor: On several occasions, Martin Luther stated that only music was second to the preaching of the word.

Choir: **May our diction be effective in communicating the sung scriptures, the spiritual songs, the anthems, the liturgy, and the hymns. We ask His blessing to allow the joy that we feel in our hearts, to literally cause our faces to glow.**

Pastor: Sing a new song to the Lord; He has done wonderful things!

Choir: **Our song is about loyalty and justice, and we sing it to our Lord.**

Pastor: Sing to the Lord, all the world! Worship the Lord with joy; come before Him with happy songs!

Choir: **Take our voices and let them sing always, only, for our King; take our lips and let them be filled with messages from thee.**

Pastor: Let us pray. Our Heavenly Father, bless this Choir in their dedication and commitment to you. Help them to remain faithful in their leadership of this congregation in worship. May all the days of their lives be joyful as they serve you well.
Help this congregation to support these musicians in their ministry of music, and in their service of love. As all of us gather here each Sunday morning, truly, may we be aware of the power and impact that music brings in assisting us to worship at the deepest levels of emotion and intellect. Keep all of our hearts to receive your Spirit, and may each one of us leave this hallowed place ready to walk in the steps of your beloved Son, Jesus. Amen.

(The Choir members may now take their usual places to sing the morning anthem.)

Choir Recognition Service

In Psalm 68 we read:
Let the righteous be joyful; let them exult before God; let them be
  jubilant with joy!
Sing to God, sing praises to His name; lift up a song to Him who
  rides upon the clouds; His name is the Lord, exult before
  Him!

Once again, we set aside a few minutes in our worship service
to demonstrate our appreciation for our choir members who have
been so consistently faithful in leading us in worship.

May I remind you that the main reason for our existence is to
lead this congregation in worship. This involves learning the hymns
and liturgy in advance, so as to make it easier for members of the
congregation to participate fully.

Our anthems and spiritual songs are selected to praise God for
His mighty acts and are a means for giving thanks for His love, His
compassion, and His grace.

We rejoice at the opportunity to serve Him each Lord's Day.
But it does take some preparation. During this season, we have
asked our faithful singers:
- to attend weekly rehearsals every Thursday evening from
  7 p.m. until 8:30 p.m.,
- to attend extra rehearsals on Saturdays to prepare for special services and major choral works,
- to sing for weekly Sunday morning worship services, and
  to arrive early to warm up and to review the selected music,
- to sing for Lenten services during the week, and/or extra
  services on Sundays, and for a few,
- to sing for the additional Contemporary Service each week.

You see here a tremendous commitment which these dedicated folks have made to our Lord Jesus, to his church, and to this
congregation.

It is my pleasure to give an award to the two singers who have attended the most rehearsals and services during the season. They are: _____ and _____.
Congratulations!

Now, even though they were not all able to be present today, I would like to read the names of all of the singers who have participated this season, and have them stand, and remain standing, so that you may know who they are. Please hold your applause until all of them have been presented.

Among our regular singers, there are some who have given extra time by carrying special responsibilities:
Librarians: _____ and _____
Attendance Secretary: _____

Here are our sopranos: Our altos:

_____   _____
_____   _____
_____   _____
_____   _____
_____

Our tenors: Our basses:

_____   _____
_____   _____
_____   _____
_____   _____
_____

And last, but certainly not least, our church organist:

_____

Please join me in showing your appreciation for their devotion and commitment this year.

(*Applause*)

(*To the Choir*) Please be seated.

There are a few other people that I would like to recognize at this time. These are wonderful folks who contribute of their time and talents other than singing to make our ministry of music a success. They are:

_____, our marvelous pianist who accompanies the choir and soloists as needed.

_____, who plays guitar for our Contemporary Service.

_____, who rings handbells for us on occasion.

_____, our lighting director who brought great drama to our Good Friday service.

_____, who built a new conductor's podium and risers for the choir.

_____, our electrician who has wired our sound system to make it and our synthesizer compatible for our Contemporary Service.

And our narrator: _____.

I trust that I have not left anyone out. If I have, I apologize.

In closing, on behalf of all of us who represent even the smallest part of the Ministry of Music in this church, I would like to extend my deepest thanks and appreciation to you, our beloved congregation, for your support and encouragement. We could not do the inspirational things which we do without your marvelous support. Many thanks.

(The Choir may now take their usual places to sing the morning anthem.)